MEMORY REWRITTEN

MEMORY REWRITTEN

Memoria y reescritura

Mariella Nigro

Translated from the Spanish by
Jesse Lee Kercheval and Jeannine Marie Pitas

WHITE PINE PRESS / BUFFALO, NEW YORK

White Pine Press
P.O. Box 236
Buffalo, NY 14201
www.whitepine.org

Publication of this book was supported by public funds from the New York State Council on the Arts, with the support of Governor Kathy Hochul and the New York State Legislature, a State Agency and the University of Wisconsin-Madison.

Acknowledgements: We would like to thank the following magazines for publishing poems that appear in the book:

Alaska Quarterly Review: "The Dark Air."
Asymptote: "Meditaciones/Meditations I, II, III," "Acciones inconclusas/ Unfinished Acts," and "Partidas/Departures I, II."
Plume: "Circularidad/Circularity," "La casa de los naranjos/The House of Orange Trees," "Niña en el campo/Girl in the Country," "Visita/Visit" and "Escribo una elegía/I'm Writing an Elegy."
World Literature Today: "La palabra y el clinamen/The word and the cli namen," "Poeta leyendo en voz alta/Poet Reading Aloud," and "Y da la lección/And He Teaches the Lesson."

Cover Image: From *Del Libro Acuarelas,* art by Cecilia Mattos and text by Mariella Nigro (Montevideo, 2005)

Printed and bound in the United States of America.

ISBN 978-1-945680-62-5

Library of Congress Control Number: 2022940637

CONTENTS

Otro orden del caos / Another Order of Chaos

Introduction

"Sister souls of mine, never look back!" admonishes Uruguayan *modernista* poet Delmira Agustini (1886-1914) in her "Elegías dulces," reminding us of the ill-fated biblical Lot's wife as well as the Orpheus of Greek mythology. But sometimes, looking back is necessary. In *Memory Rewritten* (*Memoria y reescritura*), Uruguayan poet Mariella Nigro (b. 1957) delves into the experience of grief and loss mediated by the passage of time. Wounds may heal as years go by, but that healing is itself a loss of connection with those who are gone.

Memory Rewritten is a meditation on the insufficiency of language to contain human emotion and memory—and the paradoxical reality that it is the only means we have to preserve them. Including some poems from the unpublished collection *Memoria de lo invisible* while revisiting, reexamining, and rewriting poems from earlier published work, Nigro's new collection—published here for the first time in either Spanish and English—suggests that the act of remembering ultimately involves the creation of something new.

An established presence in Montevideo's literary scene, Nigro has published nine collections of poetry and received numerous awards for her work, including the prestigious Bartolomé Hidalgo Prize for Poetry given by the Uruguayan Book Association; The Morosoli Prize awarded by the Lolita Rubial Foundation; and multiple prizes from the Uruguayan Ministry of Education and Culture. Well aware of Uruguay's long tradition of women poets, Nigro is a link in that chain, not only as a poet, but also as a critic and essayist, often writing about other women poets such as Circe Maia (b. 1932) and Ida Vitale (b. 1923).

Bringing this critical sensibility to *Memory Rewritten*, Nigro converses with her poetic peers and foremothers. lacing her own memories with epigraphs from such writers as Amanda Berenguer (1921-2010), Virginia Lucas (b. 1977), Marosa di Giorgio (1932-2004), and Tatiana Oroño (b. 1947). As she says in the note after the last poem, "This book lives by quotation, circular and eternal, searching in the uncertain memory for truth slanted by time, reduced to the succulent essence of the unsaid, or of what is better said by the poets I summon on these pages."

The poets Nigro invokes are from the center of Uruguayan literary life, not from the obscure periphery. In fact, Uruguay's major canonical poets are women. In the early twentieth century, Uruguay underwent several progressive reforms that advanced women's equality of opportunity in education and profession. Since the *fin de siècle* period of *modernismo,* when Delmira Agustini and María Eugenia Vaz Ferreira (1875-1924) were powerful voices in the first pan-Latin American literary movement, Uruguayan women have distinguished themselves as poets in every generation up to the present. Since Jeannine began translating Marosa di Giorgio and Jesse Lee began translating Circe Maia, we both have made it our mission to read, study, translate, and amplify the voices of Uruguayan women poets. Jeannine has done this by publishing five books by di Giorgio as well as translating work by Selva Casal (1927-2020) and Amanda Berenguer; Jesse Lee has done this by translating Circe Maia, Idea Vilariño (1920-2009), Tatiana Oroño, and many young women writers.

This project came to us through one of those connections. Jesse Lee met Mariella Nigro at a reading Nigro gave with Tatiana Oroño in Montevideo and then read the manuscript of *Memory Rewritten,* falling in love with it. We both appreciate the beauty of its imagery and the way in which it approaches loss, grief, and trauma. For Jeannine, having worked extensively on Marosa di Giorgio—another writer who draws heavily on childhood memory—the theme of transforming memory into poetry is fascinating, as is Nigro's reflection upon that process. Jesse Lee saw clearly the connections between the use of memory in Nigro's work and Circe Maia's.

"I'm writing an elegy / and so I'm arranging a dark bouquet of useless words / with their eloquence of broken petals / and burning in the rhetoric of embroidered leaves / the poem grows in black water / of the fragile overflowing vase," Nigro writes. The ghost of a beloved sister dead in childhood haunts these poems, as does the need for repetition, the compulsion to return to sites of loss and pain.

Rather than merely repeating memories, Nigro elegantly transforms them, just as she transforms her poetic influences into a distinct and personal voice. Ultimately, she salvages beauty from the wreckage: "In a box I locked like Eleusian mysteries the poems we'd shared the previous year under the January moon, along with the colored ribbons and glass beads that we'd fought over, now mine alone." In a poetics reminiscent of Hélène Cixous's *écriture féminine,* Nigro transforms the visceral, bodily experiences of loss into words and brings the reader along on a journey where grief does not proceed in orderly stages, where pain and healing coexist within the mess of language. Out of this emerges a poem.

— Jesse Lee Kercheval
Jeannine Marie Pitas

MEMORY REWRITTEN

Tell all the truth but tell it slant—

Emily Dickinson

Memoria de lo invisible

Porque el otoño seca las hojas
de manera bellísima:
deja en el aire las puras nervaduras,
ésas casi invisibles
en las que reparábamos apenas
y evapora esa verde sustancia que era,
para nosotros, hoja.

Ida Vitale
(De *Reducción del infinito*)

Memory of the Invisible

Because autumn dries the leaves
so beautifully:
their pure veins hanging in the air,
almost invisible,
barely noticed
evaporating that green substance that was,
for us, the leaf.

Ida Vitale
(From *Reducción del infinito*)

Circularidad

Ahí adelante espera el fulgor del abismo
el infinito horizonte destinado
los destellos finales de las cosas
los rayos de luz en la corola oscura
las hojas más altas, los frutos por caer y sus pimpollos leves

la futura sombra blanca del hijo del hijo del hijo…
su aura tan clara en la pantalla
y yo, tan anciana sosteniendo el tallo
en el holograma hermoso que imagino
en su emisión de fuego
y su ternura.

Y una posible casi segura región de escombros,
el ojo del huracán en medio del cuerpo
y su vendaval sonoro
en la patria oscura de la entraña
agorando vaya a saber qué sismo
qué tormenta solar
qué rayo que atraviese linfa y corazón
que brille así de oscuro.

Y un afluente más
de este río bravío y de revueltas aguas
donde la cama de morir antes fuera navío
y el jardín fuera sólo flor naranja
en breve semilla que volando va

bajo la luna que asciende su cuña como hoz
que acecha la entereza de los pinos
cuando es necesario ordenar el árbol y la noche
con la ausencia del hijo en la alta rama
y su faz asomando en la luna de enero.

Circularity

Up ahead the gleam of the abyss is waiting
boundless certain horizon
everything's final gleam
rays of light in the dark corolla
highest leaves, fruits about to fall with their delicate buds

the future white shadow of the son of the son of the son...
his aura so clear on the screen
and I, so old, gripping the stalk
in the lovely hologram I imagine
in his burst of fire
his tenderness.

And a possible, almost safe site of wreckage,
the eye of the hurricane at the body's center
and its echoing gale
in the dark interior country
that, prophetic, might predict what earthquake
what solar storm
what lightning bolt traversing lymph and heart
will shine in the dark.

And one more tributary
of this untamed river with rough waters
where the deathbed was once a ship
and the garden only grew orange blossoms
their brief bloom taking flight

under the moon that lifts its blade like a scythe
stalking the fortitude of the pines
when it's necessary to reorder tree and night
in the absence of the son on the high branch
with his face peeking out in the January moon.

El aire oscuro

Pero el cono de luz se invierte
e ilumina el túnel del pasado
el remoto, el antiguo, el real y el de los sueños,
reducido el tiempo a un mero instante
y el espacio a un punto
bellísimo agujero negro

y allí aparecen
los pozos y albercas luminosas
repletas de pequeñas ranas y barcos de papel
en los que sumergíamos las palmas
batiendo la alegría de la infancia

y la sombra de aquellos eucaliptus
con forma de verano
con el arbusto estirando su brazada
hasta alcanzarnos la última flor que en lo bajo arboreciera
y los destellos de los caracoles
enhebrados para colgar al cuello

y nosotras, tan hermanas, bailando
con las aladas sandalias blancas de octubre
las cintas de colores en el cabello largo
la ronda en la vereda y los saltos del juego

y la imposible sombra
apenas resplandor de lo oscuro
insospechado albur
en la invisible cara de la muerte.

The Dark Air

But the cone of light is reversed
illuminating the tunnel of the past
the remote, the old, the real, the stuff of dreams,
time compressed to a mere instant
space to a point
beautiful black hole

and wells appear
luminous pools
full of little frogs and paper boats
where we dipped our palms
splashing childhood joy

and the shadow of those eucalyptus trees
shaped like summer
with the bush stretching its arm
so we could reach the last low-growing flower
and the glimmer of snails
threaded and hung around our necks

and we, such sisters, dancing
in winged white sandals of October
colored ribbons through long hair
Ring Around the Rosie, leaping over the wall

and the impossible shade
barely a flash of darkness
unsuspected fate
in the invisible face of death.

La casa de los naranjos

que en el ámbar solar pereceremos,
a contraluz, de cara al viejo muro

. . .sitiada por un muro de altas olas,
piedra en lo blanco, blanco sobre el muro

Amanda Berenguer
(De *El río*)

Hubo un tiempo en que buscaba caracoles entre la vereda amarilla y el muro de piedra junto al que había caído mi hermana y había muerto. Los perseguía para matarlos.

Yo usaba aquella ropa legada por mandato materno, la que no fue donada, aquel bikini tejido que, de tan chico, mi pubertad modelaba, y entonces me gustaba.
Había caído en ella, en su pecho menudo, rosa, blanco y celeste, y en sus camisetas de batik, enredada entre los hilos con que habíamos enhebrado entonces caracoles en collares que debíamos despojar de un tirón cuando aparecían las asquerosas babosas recorriendo el escote.

Encerré en una caja como misterios eleusinos los poemas compartidos el último año bajo la luna de enero y las cintas de colores y los abalorios que entonces disputamos y ahora sólo a mí pertenecían (en ellos atrapada me quemaban ardiéndome en el cuello).

Luego, junto a la playa volaba un polvo blanquísimo.

En la soledad de las canteras verdes yo pensaba en su nombre y su rostro sin hueso. Y la extrañaba. Y le decía:

Soy yo, que he venido con las rosas a colgar su epitafio de corola
y la flor de ilusión que lo rubrica.

The House of Orange Trees

how will we look in the amber sun,
backlit, facing the old wall

. . .besieged by a wall of high waves,
stone over the whiteness, whiteness over the wall

Amanda Berenguer
(From *El río*)

There was a time when I looked for snails between the yellow sidewalk and the stone wall where my sister had fallen and died. I followed them in order to kill them.

I wore those clothes handed down on my mother's orders, clothes not given away, that knit bikini, so tiny it showed off my puberty, which was why I liked it.
I'd collapsed into her, her small breasts, pink, white and pale, into her batik shirts, tangled among the threads we'd strung with snails for necklaces we had to yank off when gross slugs came slithering over the neckline.

In a box I locked like Eleusinian mysteries the poems we'd shared the previous year under the January moon, along with colored ribbons and glass beads we'd fought over, now mine alone. (Trapped in them my neck got burnt, stinging).

Later, along the beach the whitest dust was flying.

In the green quarries' solitude I invoked her name and boneless face. And I missed her. And I said:

It's me, I've come with roses to hang an epitaph of petals
sealed by a hopeful flower.

No estás ahí.
No puede estarse ahí por tanto tiempo
estacada, estampada
en la estancia de la nada.

Por eso vuelvo, cada tanto,
a remover el agua
y sanar el revés rasguñado del mármol.

You're not there.
For so long no one has been there
stamped, staked
in the estate of nothingness.

Therefore I come, every so often,
to change the water
and heal the misfortune scratched in marble.

Niña en el campo

De noche, ellos cazaban palomas en el monte con unas largas varas de tacuara con un pincho en la punta.
Y mulitas, en una forma que no puedo olvidar…

Él llevaba una capa gruesa y larga, oscura, voladora.
Ondeaba la capa sobre el Land Rover, a los saltos por el camino iluminado por la luna. Le brillaban los ojos verdes y los dientes muy blancos.
(Recordaría todo aquello en otro aire, cuando leyera a Marosa entre la pedrería).

…

Y a cada trecho reverberaban las vacas, hinchadas por una fatal enfermedad.
La luna blanqueaba el cuero del anca.
Y las palomas zureaban.

Y yo era una niña.

Girl in the Country

At night, they hunted pigeons in the mountains using long bamboo poles
with pointed tips.
Armadillos too, in a way I can't forget…

He wore a long, thick cape, dark, flying.
He waved the cape over the Land Rover, bouncing down the moonlit road.
His green eyes and very white teeth were shining.
(I would remember all that later, when I read Marosa among the gems).

…

And at every turn, the cows shimmered, swollen with a fatal disease.
The moon whitened the leather of their haunches.
And the doves were cooing.

And I was a girl.

Visita

Algo me trajo hasta aquí.
Ahoga el olor artificial de la flor artificial, el campo verde inmenso.

Cae el sol y aparecen las ánimas.
Hay un rezo en el aire
hay aguas que corren por canales musgosos
flores marchitas,
vuelan ramas secas, llora una madre

y yo veo las pequeñas manos
en las pozas que batíamos en el aire
las cintas de colores en el pelo
y el salto en el juego sobre el muro

y la cara ahora tan visible de la muerte.

Visit

Something brought me here.
Suffocating the immense green field, the artificial flower's artificial smell.

The sun sets and purgatory's souls appear.
There's a prayer in the air
There are waters running through mossy canals
wilted flowers,
dry branches fly, a mother cries

and I see the little hands
in the puddles we splashed in the air
colored ribbons in our hair
and our game of leaping over the wall

and the now all-too-visible face of death.

Agua negra de las palabras

Black Water of Words

La palabra y el clinamen

I.

La poesía se estrella en el clinamen de la página.
Así, corro como un tren ciego y quedo empalada por el tiempo.

Antes navegaba desde el cenit al nadir del cuerpo
prendida a su eje vertical junto al vacío.
Era la rosa. Toda mojada.

Ahora es sólo la raíz, y de golpe todo el árbol.
Y la sequedad de la rama. Y lo innombrable del mucílago.

The Word and the Clinamen

I.

Poetry crashes into the clinamen of the page.
So I run like a blind train and get impaled by time.

Before I sailed from the zenith to the nadir of the body
pinned to its vertical axis beside the void.
It was the rose. All wet.

Now it is only the root, and suddenly the whole tree.
And the dryness of the branch. And the unnamable mucilage.

II.

En la prosa va el fuego
y fénix
al pensamiento en llamas
le sale el ala de la poesía

y luego vuela hacia la lumbre de los ojos
y se inunda en la oscuridad:
ceguera, mudez y vaciamiento del poema.

Apenas puedo arrojar a la tierra la piedra de la voz.

Tiembla la raíz del cuerpo
y queda en la rama la palabra partida.

Entonces,
soy un árbol desnudo.

II.

In prose goes fire
and phoenix
to burning thought
comes the wing of poetry

and later it flies toward the eyes' fire
and floods in the darkness:
blindness, muteness and a hollowed-out poem.

I can barely throw the voice's stone to the ground.

The body's root trembles
and the split word remains on the branch.

Then, I am a tree,
naked.

Escribo una elegía

y formo así un oscuro ramo
de inútiles palabras
con su elocuencia de quebrado pétalo

y ardiendo en la retórica de sus hojas bordadas
crece el poema en el agua negra
del frágil vaso desbordado:

Ay, madre,
quedó tan chiquita,

la veo allí perdida
entre el vapor blanco de las flores
y la lustrosa rigidez de la madera,
solita,

mirando hacia adentro
vaya a saber qué alto punto del cielo.

I'm Writing an Elegy

and so I'm arranging a dark bouquet
of useless words
with their eloquence of broken petals

and burning in the rhetoric of embroidered leaves
the poem grows in black water
of the fragile overflowing vase:

Ay, mother,
you were so little,

I see you lost there
between the flower's white vapor
and the wood's lustrous rigidity,
all by yourself,

looking within
toward who knows what high point of heaven.

Misiva

Escucha y mira hacia acá adentro.
Te hablo desde este lado, donde no llega la luz de la luna
y aun así hay un musgo plateado
que crece de este lado de la piel
corredores donde brillan los fuegos fatuos de los huesos
y suenan los ríos de sangre y linfa.
Acá, en esta comarca de pequeños sucesos
aleteos, brincos, estremecimientos, dudas.
Y un amasijo de venas
que la ortopedia sortea triunfalmente.

Y en medio de esta maraña tomo la navaja del deseo,
aquella llave que todo lo abría, varilla de rabdomante,
hoz con que acometo este muro que me separa del afuera
desesperado pico que desde adentro cava
desterrona dendritas
remueve escarchas del alma fría
y del pensamiento.
(Si es que escuchas el discurso visceral
para los demás audible apenas).

Con el zureo de mi ahogada libertad
tiendo las manos como palomas.
Y me las tomas.

Pero yo sigo por dentro mi relato infinito.

Missive

Listen and look inside.
I speak to you from this side, where the moonlight does not reach
and still there's a silver moss
that grows on this side of the skin
corridors where the will-o'-the-wisps of the bones shine
and rivers of blood and lymph ring.
Here, in this region of small events
tremors, starts, shiver, doubts.
And a jumble of veins
that orthopedics handles triumphantly.

And amid this tangle I take the dagger of desire,
that key that opened everything, dowsing rod,
scythe I use to attack this wall that separates me from outside
desperate beak that digs from within
unearths dendrites
rakes frost from the cold soul
and from thought.
(If you listen to the visceral speech
barely audible to others).

With the cooing of my drowned freedom
I hold out my hands like doves.
And you take them from me.

But I follow my infinite story from within.

Poeta leyendo en voz alta

Abrir palabra por palabra el páramo,
Abrirnos y mirar hacia la significante abertura...:

Ida Vitale
(De *Trema*)

Apenas inclinada
la cabeza brilla en su constancia
con el ojo encendido.

Junto al libro que una mano sostiene
la otra da su vuelo, viene y va, tiembla,
abre la puerta enorme
por donde la poesía entra

vertical, hacia la boca,
enramada donde revolotean pájaros
muelles plumas que el aliento arremolina
en el inundado pozo del poema.
Al escribir, cavó un pozo la palabra
para el cuerpo del poema
nacido como un hijo.

Ahora está el libro abierto
con los dones de la voz
que donan el amparo a la escritura,

y al leer,
el ser que se va abriendo.

Poet reading aloud

> *To open the wasteland word for word,*
> *Open ourselves and look toward the opening that signifies...*
>
> Ida Vitale
> (From *Trema*)

Barely bowed
the head shines in its steadfastness
with a lit eye.

Beside the book a hand holds
the other hand takes flight, comes and goes, trembles,
opens the enormous door
where poetry enters

up toward the mouth,
entwined branches where birds flutter,
supple feathers that breath ripples
in the flooded well of the poem.
Written, the word dug the well
for the body of the poem
born like a son.

Now the book is open
with the voice's gifts
that offer refuge to writing,

and to reading,
the being that is opened.

Reescrituras

Rewritings

La veladura del tul

I.

Entonces era la poesía que labraba en la soledad del día su espléndida grava, luego echaba su flor al pie de cada noche. Sólo dejaba surco al ser leída.
Así de simple, vegetal y espléndida era.

Antes era de fuego cuando incendiaba tu oído mi lengua crepitante, jadeo encendido de mi labia (y se quemaban los papeles al borde de la cama).

Pero ahora quiebro la vena en el rincón y la palabra deja su menudencia junto a una pared ocultamente mía; así empieza y continúa el día.
Las palabras quedan siempre lastimadas hacia atrás, con la fractura expuesta como en un débil astrágalo, y recompuestas en el aire, haciendo fe en la curvatura de la mano.
Si tejen un encaje de alabastro, queda el poema encerrado en una caja blanca con instrucciones para entender tristes huesos astillados.

Ahora los huesos van doliendo un poco más cerca de su nervadura
y otra vez hay algo que aparece y en un tris ya no canta.

Decir lo mínimo; pensarlo apenas. Casi muda.
Y lo innombrable sigue creciendo.

The Tulle Veil

I.

Then poetry was carving its splendid grave in the day's solitude, casting its flowers at the foot of each night. When read, it left only a furrow.
That was how simple, vegetal and splendid it was.

Before it was fire, when my crackling tongue, the incendiary gasp of my lips ignited your ear (and papers burned at the edge of the bed).

But now I break the vein in the corner and the word leaves its insignificance next to a wall secretly mine; in this way the day begins and continues.
The words are always wounded backwards, with the fracture exposed as in a weak ankle, and mended in the air, signed and sealed with the curve of the hand.
If the words weave an alabaster lace, the poem is enclosed in a white box with instructions for understanding sad, splintered bones.

Now the bones hurt a little closer to the veins
and again something appears and in one breath no longer sings.

Say the least; barely think about it. Almost silent.
And the unnamable continues to grow.

II.

El vestido resplandecía.
Era el pensamiento palpable del cuerpo, la palabra muda de un modelo interior, el vestido era el espejo de la soledad del ser, parábola o veladura del alma, gesto de la piel. Y el desnudo: el silencio del vestido, la amnesia del cuerpo.

Hervía la sangre, la boca rezumaba magníficas palabras. Y orlaba el vestido.
El pensamiento ardía, joven, cavilaba, enhiesto entre las sábanas, imaginaba horizontes verticales, deseaba.

Ahora, el vestido muere en el armario.

II.

The dress shimmered.
It was the body's palpable thought, the interior model's mute word; the dress was the mirror of being's loneliness, a parable or veil of the soul, a gesture of skin. And the nude: silence of the dress, body's amnesia.

The blood boiled, the mouth bled magnificent words. And embellished the dress.
The thought burned, young, brooding, erect between the sheets; it imagined vertical horizons, it desired.

Now the dress dies in the closet.

III.

De viaje
hacia la terminal del habla
sigo en el mismo sitio
de silencio inundado
saboteada en la frontera de la página
insistiendo con la letra
como en la llanura seca
inclinado y cargado de semillas
un terco labriego.

Partes de mí, desde mi centro disparadas
mis palabras
van dejando los huecos
que recogen el agua de mis hijos

aquel que se prendió a la red
y los otros que se ahogaron en la malograda zanja.

Pero estos días son frases largas,
prosodia absurda sin cesuras.
Arrastran por pasillos
su lengua indescifrable,
buscando el calor en las ventanas
si apenas logra el espesor del llanto
la inútil letanía.

No he podido sacar del carey
sino unos jugos derramados,
cosas de mí sin nombre,
vanas formas
en el fallido diseño del sueño
de mi metamorfosis.

III.

Traveling
toward the terminus of speech
I stay in the same place
of flooded silence
sabotaged at the border of the page
insisting with the letter
as if a stubborn farmworker
on the dry plain
sloping and heavy with seeds.

Parts of me, shot from my center
my words
keep leaving grooves
that collect the water of my children

the one who caught the net
and the others who drowned in the blighted ditch.

But these days are long sentences
absurd prosody without caesuras.
They drag their indecipherable language
down hallways,
looking for warmth in the windows
barely achieving the density of a cry
a useless litany.

I haven't managed to cast off the shell
except for some spilled juice,
nameless parts of me,
vain forms
in the failed design of the dream
of my metamorphosis.

IV.

En el autorretrato apócrifo de la soñadora
había de todo
pinceles papeles broches
mucho cordel para liar lo inasible
el pensamiento como un cristal roto
cortando por dentro
y un yo partido colgando del costado.

Piensa—decía—en la primera frontera,
cómo llegaste a nacer,
librándote entre sangre de tanto envoltorio.

El sueño es un cristal que lleva
al otro lado de la cama
allá donde el corazón hace agua
en la ribera de la nada.
Y la escritura cortada cuelga de un libro en blanco
porque vive por sí misma
segada y cegada en el cristal del vaso
ahogada en su alimento de agua negra.

De noche crece una flor
de largo tallo
que en el día se acorta
como un sueño.

Vuelve a ser apenas la misma
si al despertar
(con esquirlas de espejo y estigma de sirena)
muestra la cortada de cristales.

IV.

In the fabled self-portrait of the dreamer
there was everything
brushes papers brooches
string to bundle the ungraspable
a thought like a broken crystal
cut from within
and a broken me hanging from the side.

Think—she said—about the first frontier,
how you came to be born,
amid blood, freeing you from so much wrapping.

The dream is a crystal that takes you
to the other side of the bed
there where the heart makes water
on the shore of nothingness.
And the clipped writing hangs from a blank book
because it lives on its own
reaped and blinded in the glass's crystal
drowned in its sustenance of black water.

At night a long-stemmed
flower grows
and in the day it's shortened
like a dream.

She is just the same again
if awakening
(with mirror's splinters and siren's stigma)
she shows the cut of the crystals.

V.

He cifrado el cuerpo
detrás de la palabra.
Si goza la escritura de todos los excesos,
si al padecer ordena,
si dirige con esmero la tragedia.
Si sufre.

Hiere el espacio
el filo del silencio
y en los cortes
se ahogan las rutinas vanas
del trámite de vivir.
Si piensa.
Si llora.
Si enciende la voz,
Si escribe el cuerpo.

Grávido, el espejo profana lo sagrado,
roba sustancia al dar a luz la carne
por empujar a la poesía con sus aguas
hacia el rincón lunar de la escritura.
Si entra en el libro tanto reflejo,
si resiste tanta luz.
O queda tras el tul
el breve infante de lo escrito.
Si nace hábil.
Si sobrevive el poema
con tanto desconcierto.

V.

I have encrypted the body
behind the word.
If writing revels in all its excesses,
if, enduring, it orders,
if it carefully directs the tragedy.
If it suffers.

The blade of silence
wounds the space
and with each cut
petty routines drown
in the business of living.
If it thinks.
If it cries.
If it illuminates the voice,
If it writes the body.

Pregnant, the mirror profanes the sacred,
steals substance by giving birth to flesh
by pushing the waters of poetry
toward the lunar corner of writing.
If so much reflection enters the book,
if it resists so much light.
Or if the brief infant of the written
remains behind the tulle.
If it is born clever.
If the poem survives
with so much bewilderment.

Sonetos después del nombre

I.

No queda palabra ni predicado
que no dijera ya la letanía
de madre a hijo en la hendidura viva
del mismo libro subrayado.

No queda sustantivo ni enredado
verso que no llegara a su afonía
línea que no agotara su sangría
nombre que no quedara desmayado.

Este equívoco sentido que me enmienda
este verbo que ayer he conjugado
este decir que acaso me desdice;

es la poesía que la lengua incendia
son los silencios que en algo me rediment,
esto que apenas digo ha caducado.

Sonnets after the Name

I.

There remains no word or predicate
that doesn't speak the litany
of mother to child in the living crack
of the same underlined book.

There remains no noun or knotted
verse that doesn't lose its voice
or line that doesn't exhaust its margin
or name that doesn't faint.

This mistaken sense that corrects me
this verb I conjugated yesterday
this utterance that perhaps unsays me;

it's poetry the tongue sets on fire
silences that somehow redeem me,
this thing I barely say has expired.

II.

El eje refulgente ahí en el centro
donde comprime al numen la armadura
de la palabra, esa rosa menuda
con su ojiva en el minúsculo templo.

Menudencia ingrávida el reflejo
de la rosa de corola oscura
muestra a veces en su carcasa dura
el poema comprimido hasta el vértigo.

He llegado a ver entrelíneas
del poema alumbrando la rosa
la llamita final del soneto;

sombra roja en la palabra nívea,
cómo filtra la tumba celosa
si se entreabre el redil de los huesos.

II.

The gleaming axis there in the center
where the numen presses the framework
of the word, that tiny rose
with its Gothic arch in the tiny temple.

A weightless trifle, the reflection
of the rose with its dark corolla
shows at times in its hard casing
the poem compressed to vertigo.

I've come to read between the lines
of the poem that lights up the rose
the sonnet's small, final flame;

a red shadow in the snow-white word,
how it screens the jealous tomb
should the bones' enclosure open.

III.

Es la palabra un pájaro menudo
con su zumbido hacia el papel del cielo
su ala se incendia en su ligero vuelo
y la frase en llamas deja al verbo oscuro.

Nombrar lo que no existe es tan absurdo,
queda temblando el pájaro suspenso,
insondable saeta tras el vuelo
del poema, como un pobre árbol desnudo.

He atrapado lo innombrable con el pájaro,
he fraseado en su zumbido lo más puro,
le he engarzado la piedra de la voz:

imbebible es el agua de su cántaro,
en el aire lo he partido con la hoz
del silencio de este verso que murmuro.

III.

The word is a tiny bird
humming toward the sky's paper
its wing on fire in gentle flight
and the flaming phrase leaves behind the dark word.

To name the non-existent is so absurd,
the suspended bird is left trembling,
inscrutable arrow in the poem's
flight, like a poor naked tree.

I have trapped the unnamable with the bird,
I have made the purest phrases in its hum,
I have set the stone of its voice:

the water from its jug is undrinkable
in the air I have smashed it with the scythe
of silence in this verse whisper.

IV.

Caen palabras desde el suero a nombrar
aquello malherido que el cuerpo calla.
Vienen de velo abierto en la garganta
con su blancura obscena a silenciar

todo aquello que se pudo imaginar
todo lo que en el sueño encalla
como un barco siniestro que en la playa
arrojara los secretos de alta mar.

El viento del silencio las desnuda
y apenas se les ve al traspasar
el vaho de la química del sueño;

horadan con su trágica blancura
la cama de hospital, y en el silencio
terminan revelando la verdad.

IV.

Words fall from serum when naming
that injured man silenced by the body.
They come with an open veil from the throat
to silence with obscene whiteness

all that could be imagined
all that dreams run aground
like a sinister ship on the beach
that might toss the high seas' secrets.

The wind of silence undresses them
and you hardly see them running through
the mist of the dreams' chemistry;

with their tragic whiteness they pierce
the hospital bed, and in the silence
they end up revealing the truth.

Otro orden del caos

A ese desborde, en su orden
solo puedes decirle: fatalidad del poema.
Su único revés, esto que queda de ti.

Virginia Lucas
(De *El sonido del viento entre las nubes*)

Another Order out of Chaos

To that outburst, in its place
you can only say: the poem's bad luck.
Its only setback, this is what's left of you.

Virginia Lucas
(From *El sonido del viento entre las nubes*)

Meditaciones

I.

La pregunta da vueltas y vueltas
y crea un pensamiento oscuro, una idea
que no se convence a sí misma de su blancura.

Qué, por qué, quién, cuándo, cómo, dónde,
frutos que cuelgan del árbol del deseo,
flores caídas o semillas suspendidas en el aire.

Luego, viento que las lleva lejos,
polen que fertiliza otras preguntas
en tierra yerma.

Y que nadie contesta.

Meditations

I.

The question goes round and round
and creates a dark thought, an idea
that doesn't convince itself of its whiteness.

What, why, who, when, how, where,
fruits that hang from the tree of desire,
fallen flowers or seeds suspended in the air.

Later, the wind carries them away,
pollen fertilizes other questions
in barren land.

And nobody answers.

II.

...se le formaban pensamientos
como flores en la sien...

Marosa di Giorgio
(De *Misales*)

Vuelvo una y otra vez al mismo árbol
bajo los frutos recientes, las altas flores
los rizomas y raíces a la vista
los ramajes caídos.

Todos, pensamientos de la misma dehesa
donde ideas pastan en soledad y crecen
hasta soltar sus gemas de infértil galladura.

Desmalezo el terreno, día a día, tarea
en el albur del débil pastoreo
de enmarañadas ideas sin cosecha.

Y quedo con un humilde ramo de flores
enjoyando la cabeza.

II.

. . .if thoughts formed
like flowers at your temple. . .

Marosa di Giorgio
(From *Misales*)

I return again and again to the same tree
under the new fruits, the high flowers
the rhizomes and roots in sight
the fallen branches.

All of them, thoughts from the same meadow
where ideas graze in solitude and grow
until they release their buds, infertile eggs.

I weed the ground, day after day, a task
at the whim of weak grazing
of tangled ideas without harvest.

And I am left with a humble bouquet of flowers
bejeweling my head.

III.

Si piensa en el amor y en el orden de las cosas
como Delmira
si la primera fuente es el último linde
y la gota final ya manó en el inicio,

hacia atrás el resplandor y el estruendo mudo,
hacia adelante la luz tenue y el eco,
hoy mismo: el asombro, el azar,
la luna menguante
y la flor de pie roto. Como Delmira.

Entonces, ¿qué puerta de qué casa me clausura,
qué viento de qué calle me libera,
qué blanco de qué página me escribe?

III.

If you think about love and the order of things
like Delmira
if the first source is the last boundary
and the final drop already flowed at the beginning,

back toward the radiance and the mute roar,
forward toward the dim light and echo,
today: amazement, chance,
the waning moon
and the standing flower broken. Like Delmira.

So, what door of what house encloses me,
what wind from what street frees me,
what white of what page writes me?

La nada

Nada es la Nada, que no puede pensarse

Circe Maia
(De *Dualidades*)

Estado actual del pensamiento: una pavesa que todo lo incinera, y luego se apaga y se olvida.

Nothingness

Nothing is the Nothingness that can't be conceived of.

Circe Maia
(From *Dualidades*)

Current state of thought: an ember that could burn up everything, later extinguished and forgotten.

Y da la lección

provista de los avíos del vivir…
la abuela hace el camino de la vida repleta de nadas…

Tatiana Oroño
(De *Estuario*)

Le he leído el poema a Marco
y él supo señalar una a una las letras de su nombre
en el agua del espejo de mi ojo

y repitió la rima
trinando ante el asombro
de las correspondencias
dejando un pajarito dentro de mi cabeza.

Que viva en mi ojo y en mi árbol trine
y reciba en los versos
los avíos del vivir.

Después, lea,
sepa ver el brillo del agua del poema,
su sentido, en la hermosa enramada de las letras.

Sea la alta flor que sostiene mi árbol.

And She Teaches the Lesson

Given the provisions for living...
the grandmother takes life's journey full of nothings...

Tatiana Oroño
(from *Estuario*)

I have read the poem to Marco
and he knew how to point out his name's letters one by one
in the water of the mirror of my eye

and he repeated the rhyme
trilling in amazement
at the correspondences
leaving a little bird inside my head.

May it live in my eye and trill in my tree
and receive in verse
the provisions for living.

Then, may it read,
see the shining water of the poem,
its meaning in the lovely bower of letters.

Be the tall flower that sustains my tree.

Acciones inconclusas

En el sueño, digo una oración larguísima mientras giro en mi danza de derviche y vuelo; en la vigilia, estoy muda y clavada a la tierra.
En el sueño encuentro la verdad; en la vigilia, dudo.

*

Voy manejando bajo la lluvia; los limpiaparabrisas enjugan las lágrimas del vidrio.
Pero sigue en mis ojos toda el agua.

*

Hoy el volcán Popocatépetl está lanzando humo y ascuas.
Está encendido también dentro de mí, porque sigo sentada en una silla extrañamente inclinada y siguen oscilando los pendientes de jade, mientras ruge el volcán del Cerro de Montevideo.
Y yo enderezo la columna regiamente.

*

(Dicen que el desierto de Atacama se ha llenado de flores violetas pero yo estoy aquí con la hoz en este erial estéril donde mutilo los pequeños brotes de mi árbol.)

*

Amo lo redondo, la hermosa pregnancia
de la plateada esfera de Parménides.
Pero no esta ciliada esfera colorida
con su corona de lata y alfileres
que día a día acecha en la ventana.

Unfinished Acts

While sleeping, I say a long prayer while I whirl in my dervish dance and fly; while awake, I am mute and pinned to the ground.
While sleeping I encounter truth; while awake, I doubt.

☆

I go driving in the rain; windshield wipers dry the tears of that glass.
But all the water in my eyes is still there.

☆

Today the Popocatépetl volcano is spewing out smoke and embers.
It's also catching fire inside me, because I'm still seated on a strangely leaning chair, and my jade earrings keep swinging as the volcano of Montevideo's Cerro roars.
And I straighten my back royally.

☆

(They say the Atacama Desert has filled with purple flowers but I am here with my scythe in this sterile wasteland where I destroy my tree's tiny buds.)

☆

I love the roundness, the gorgeous allure
of Parmenides' silver-plated sphere.
But not this colorful sphere with its cilia
with its crown of tin and pins
that stalks me every day in the window.

Partidas

A Agustín

I.

Hay un círculo de fuego que va a ser traspasado
como una nave hacia el espacio disparada
y estarás más fuerte que en el fórceps del alumbramiento

Mi pensamiento irá así de lejos
y allí estaré sin que lo sepas

y estaré aquí
de a poco, intermitentemente
siguiendo la línea que viene desde la empolladura

Ahora emerge el adiós como una rasgadura
y los jirones al aire te acompañan
y lo harán por siempre

Mientras sigas mirando hacia el cielo
aunque no veas la Cruz del Sur
habrá algún punto que hacia ti mi luz refracte

y estaré como una marca indeleble en tu mapa
entre el agua y la sangre
dibujándose.

Departures

To Agustín

I.

There's a circle of fire you're about to run through
like a ship shot through space
and you will be stronger than in the forceps of childbirth

My thought will go far away
And I'll be there without you knowing

and I'll be here
little by little, sporadically
following the line from the brooding nest

Now the farewell breaks out like a rip
and the shreds go with you into the air
and they always will

While you keep looking up at the sky
though you can't see the Southern Cross
there will be a point when my light refracts toward you

and I'll be there like an indelible mark on your map
drawing itself
between water and blood.

II.

Hay un avistamiento que no es de pájaro
es de hijo a lo lejos
es un adivinamiento de su vuelo
una raíz al aire, al viento del sur
que hace volar la lengua materna
y la deja perdida al borde de un río marrón
al que no llega el agua de los canales.

Espero llegar a ver sus flores y los colores de su amanecer.
Recordarle que soy el tallo.
Y el tronco de su árbol.
Y sus hojas caducas.

Cinco horas antes le llegará el sol.
Leerá cinco horas después mi último poema.

II.

There's a sighting not of birds
but of a distant son
it's a divination of their flight
a root in air, a wind from the South
that makes the mother tongue fly
and leaves it lost at a brown river's edge
that the canals' water won't reach.

I hope to come and see his flowers and dawn colors.
To remind him that I am the stem.
And the trunk of his tree.
And his deciduous leaves.

Five hours earlier the sun will rise.
Five hours later he will read my last poem.

Nota

Este libro recoge textos del libro inédito *Memoria de lo invisible* (tercer premio en la categoría poesía inédita de los Premios Nacionales de Literatura del Ministerio de Educación y Cultura, edición 2018) y otros de diferente data, algunos reescritos, otros surgidos al escribir algún ensayo. *Los Sonetos después del nombre* dan forma de soneto, respectivamente, a los poemas *Poesía VI, I, III y IV* del libro *Después del nombre (Estuario,* 2011, Premio Bartolomé Hidalgo 2011). Tal vez, como en el ensayo, este libro vive por una cita circular y eterna, buscando en la incierta memoria la verdad escorada por el tiempo, reducido a la jugosa esencia de lo no dicho, o de lo dicho mejor por las poetas que en estas páginas convoco.

Mariella Nigro

Note

This book gathers together texts from the unpublished book *Memoria de lo invisible* (which won the third prize in the unpublished poetry category of the National Literature Awards of the Ministry of Education and Culture of Uruguay, *2018*) with others from different dates, some rewritten, others that emerged while attempting an essay. The *Sonnets after the name* give sonnet form, respectively, to the poems "Poesía VI, I, III and IV" of the book *After the name (Estuario,* 2011, Bartolomé Hidalgo Award 2011). Perhaps, as in an essay, an attempt, this book lives by quotation, circular and eternal, searching in the uncertain memory for truth slanted by time, reduced to the succulent essence of the unsaid, or of what is better said by the poets I summon on these pages.

—Mariella Nigro

The Author

Mariella Nigro (Montevideo, Uruguay, 1957) is a lawyer, poet and essayist. She has published ten books of poetry and two of literary essays including: *Impresionante Frida. Poemario al óleo* (Biblioteca de Marcha, Montevideo, 1997), *Mujer en construcción* (Vintén, Montevideo, 2000), *Umbral del cuerpo* (La Gotera, Colección Hermes Criollo, Montevideo, 2003), *El río vertical* (Artefato, Montevideo, 2005), *El tiempo circular* (Yaugurú, Montevideo, 2009), *Después del nombre* (Estuario, Montevideo, 2011), *Orden del caos* (Vitruvio, Madrid, 2016), *Frida y México. De visiones y miradas* (Yaugurú, Montevideo, 2017) and *Autorretrato. Una antología personal,* (Librería Linardi y Risso, 2022). In 2011, she received the Bartolomé Hidalgo Poetry Prize and in 2013 the Morosoli Prize, awarded by the Lolita Rubial Foundation, both honoring her complete poetic work.

The Translators

Jesse Lee Kercheval is a poet, writer, and translator, specializing in Uruguayan poetry. Her translations include *Still Life with Defeats* by Tatiana Oroño, also published by White Pine Press, *Love Poems* by Idea Vilariño and *The Invisible Bridge: Selected Poems of Circe Maia.* She is the co-translator, with Jeannine Marie Pitas, of *A Sea at Dawn* by Silvia Guerra. She is the Zona Gale Professor Emerita of English at the University of Wisconsin-Madison and the coeditor of the Wisconsin Poetry Series at the University of Wisconsin Press.

Jeannine Marie Pitas is a teacher, writer and Spanish-English translator originally from Buffalo, NY. She has translated or co-translated nine previous books of poetry, most recently *A Sea at Dawn* by Silvia Guerra (also co-translated with Jesse Lee Kercheval), published by Eulalia Books. She is Spanish Translation editor for *Presence: A Journal of Catholic Poetry,* and she teaches at Saint Vincent College in Latrobe, PA.

The Cliff Becker Book Prize in Translation

> "Translation is the medium through which American readers gain greater access to the world. By providing us with as direct a connection as possible to the individual voice of the author, translation provides a window into the heart of a culture."
>
> —Cliff Becker, May 16, 2005

Cliff Becker (1964–2005) was the National Endowment for the Arts Literature Director from 1999 to 2005. He began his career at the NEA in 1992 as a literature specialist, was named Acting Director in 1997, and in 1999 became the NEA's Director of Literature.

The publication of this book of translation is a reflection of Cliff's passionate belief that the arts must be accessible to a wide audience and not subject to vagaries of the marketplace. During his tenure at the NEA, he expanded support for individual translators and led the development of the NEA Literature Translation Initiative. His efforts did not stop at the workplace, however. He carried his passion into the kitchen as well as into the board room. Cliff could often be seen at home relaxing in his favorite, worn-out, blue T-shirt, which read, "Art Saves Me!" He truly lived by this credo.

To ensure that others got the chance to have their lives impacted by uncensored art, Cliff hoped to create a foundation to support the literary arts which would not be subject to political changes or fluctuations in patronage, but would be marked solely for the purpose of supporting artists, and in particular, the creation and distribution of art which might not otherwise be available. While he could not achieve this goal in his short life, seven years after his untimely passing, his vision was realized.

The Cliff Becker Endowment for the Literary Arts was established by his widow and daughter in 2012 to give an annual publication prize in translation in his memory. The Cliff Becker Book Prize in Translation annually produces one volume of literary translation in English. It is our hope that with ongoing donations to help grow the Becker Endowment for the Literary Arts, important artists will continue to touch, and perhaps save, lives of those whom they reach through the window of translation.

Donations to The Cliff Becker Endowment for the Literary Arts will help ensure that Cliff 's vision continues to enrich our literary heritage. It is more important than ever before that English-speaking readers are able to comprehend our world and our histories through the literatures of diverse cultures. Tax deductible donations to the Endowment will be gratefully received by White Pine Press. Checks should be made payable to White Pine Press and sent to The Cliff Becker Endowment for the Literary Arts, c/o White Pine Press, P.O. Box 236, Buffalo, NY 14201.

Cliff Becker Book Prize in Translation

Memory Rewritten - Mariella Nigro. Translated by Jesse Lee Kercheval and Jeannine Marie Pitas, 2023.

The Beginning of Water - Tran Le Khanh. Translated by the author and Bruce Weigl. 2021

Hatchet - Carmen Boullosa. Translated by Lawrence Schimel. 2020

Bleeding from All 5 Senses - Mario Santiago Papasquiaro. Translated by Cole Heinowitz. 2019

The Joyous Science: Selected Poems - Maxim Amelin. Translated by Derek Mong & Anne O. Fischer. 2018

Purifications or the Sign of Retaliation - Myriam Fraga. Translated by Chloe Hill. 2017

Returnings: Poems of Love & Distance - Rafael Alberti. Translated by Carolyn L. Tipton. 2016

The Milk Underground - Ronny Someck. Translated by Hana Inbar & Robert Manaster. 2015

Selected Poems of Mikhail Yeryomin. Translated by J. Kates. 2014

A Hand Full of Water - Tzveta Sofronieva. Translated by Chantel Wright. 2012